Collins

Broads
Park R
Favourite walks

Published by Collins
An imprint of HarperCollins*Publishers*
Westerhill Road, Bishopbriggs, Glasgow G64 2QT
collins.reference@harpercollins.co.uk
www.harpercollins.co.uk

HarperCollins*Publishers*
1st Floor, Watermarque Building, Ringsend Road, Dublin 4, Ireland

Printed in Bosnia and Herzegovina

ISBN   978-0-00-846272-7   10 9 8 7 6 5 4 3 2 1

MIX
Paper from
responsible sources
FSC™ C007454

This book is produced from independently certified FSC™ paper
to ensure responsible forest management.

For more information visit: www.harpercollins.co.uk/green

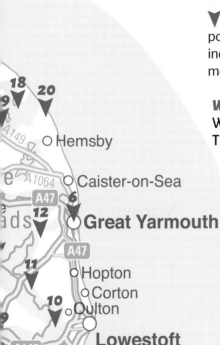

WALK 18
Horsey Mere, River Thurne, *page 112*

WALK LOCATIONS

▼ Recommended starting point for each route – refer to individual walk instructions for more details.

WALK 20
Winterton-on-Sea, River Thurne area, *page 122*

WALK 19
Potter Heigham, River Thurne, *page 116*

WALK 15 Upton, River Bure, *page 96*

WALK 6 Halvergate Marshes and Berney Arms, River Yare, *page 44*

WALK 12 Burgh Castle, River Waveney, *page 78*

WALK 5
Reedham, River Yare, *page 38*

WALK 11 Herringfleet Hills, River Waveney, *page 72*

WALK 10 Carlton Marshes, River Waveney, *page 68*

Introduction

Water, air and wide-open spaces – the Broads is the UK's only wetland National Park, made up of seven rivers and their floodplains, covering a total of 117 square miles (303 sq km) in east Norfolk and north Suffolk. The walks in this guide are all close to the seven rivers, the Bure, Ant and Thurne in the Northern Broads and the Wensum, Yare, Chet and Waveney in the Southern Broads.

With over 60 broads and other areas of open water as well – estuary, lake, mere, 'water', pond, pool, scrape, decoy, dyke, cut, sound, canal, flood – and a small part of the Broads adjoining the coast, you are always conscious that distinctions between land and water are fluid.

The areas of water known as broads were created by medieval peat diggers during the ninth-13th centuries, when peat was dug out to use as fuel for heating and cooking. Later, water levels rose, the peat diggings flooded and broad areas of water were formed. Most of the peat diggings were abandoned by the 14th century and later, the broads were widely thought to be natural lakes. It wasn't until the 1950s that scientific research was carried out and Dr Joyce Lambert established that they were man-made.

Spreading out from the waterways are reed and sedge fens, wet woodland known as carr and lush grazing marshes offering immense views of open skies and opportunities for stargazing under dark skies. The Broads habitats support an incredible quarter of the UK's rarest wildlife including the huge swallowtail butterfly and the Norfolk hawker dragonfly, both rarely found outside the Broads. Rare bitterns make their booming call from the fens, otters have made a comeback, marsh harriers soar overhead and the dawn chorus makes you truly appreciate that there's a wild other world out there. White water lilies, flag irises, marsh marigolds and rare fen orchids are among the distinctive flowers of the Broads, while the reeds offer an ever-changing background from green in the spring, through the purple heads of summer and on to the rusty tones of autumn and the gold of their winter harvest.

Set in this landscape are features closely associated with it – the sails of mills, yachts and wherries. Drainage mills, also known as windpumps, were built to drain the marshes dry enough for cattle grazing. Many of the remaining mills have been restored and are open to visitors. Likewise the wherries, originally built as cargo boats, but adapted to pleasure use in Victorian and Edwardian times when waterborne trade declined. Eight wherries remain and seven of them provide visiting and sailing opportunities.

The Broads offers all kinds of water activities on its 125 miles (200 km) of navigable waterways: day hire and holiday boats with motor or sails; canoeing, kayaking and paddleboarding; large and small boat trips and ferries. There are several places offering accessible boating suitable for wheelchair users.

Go to **www.VisitTheBroads.co.uk** for everything you need to make the most of your visit, including where to stay on land and water, where to enjoy the best of local produce and full details of places to visit.

Getting around

Walking, boating and cycling are all great ways for getting around the Broads. If you're driving, car parking charges may apply.

For boaters, many of the walks in this guide are close to Broads Authority (BA) 24-hour free moorings; other moorings are available too but there may be charges. For cyclists, National Route 1 runs south from Norwich city centre out into the Broads. For all bus services in the Broads go to Traveline 0871 200 22 33 **www.traveline.info.**

Train travel can really expand your views. The Bittern Line and the Wherry Lines can make more places accessible for walking without road travel, especially sites like the wonderful expanses of grazing marshes, and you can see how the landscape changes as you travel. The Wherry Lines go east from Norwich to Great Yarmouth and Lowestoft. The Bittern Line goes north from Norwich through Wroxham to Sheringham on the North Norfolk coast. More details from **www.bitternline.com, www.wherrylines. com,** Greater Anglia 0345 600 7245 **www.greateranglia.co.uk** or National Rail Enquiries 03457 48 49 50 **www.nationalrail.co.uk.**

With so much wildlife in the Broads, some of the walks in this guide are on or partially on nature reserves. Those with walks included in this guide are free entry, but donations are always appreciated. Many don't allow access for dogs. Please check opening times and other details where appropriate – many reserves are open dawn to dusk, varying with the time of year.

On some walks you may like to allow extra time for visits to places on or close to the walk, and you may like to add time for longer stops on longer walks. Please check opening times with places you plan to visit (many places open seasonally). Distances and times given are approximate.

For further exploring, the Broads has 190 miles (300 km) of public footpaths. As well as many other shorter walks there are long-distance routes too. The Weavers' Way passes through the Northern Broads and then goes on to North Norfolk, the Norfolk Coast Path takes you through the Broads at Horsey and Winterton, the Wherryman's Way follows the River Yare from Norwich to Great Yarmouth, and the Angles Way goes south from Great Yarmouth and into the Suffolk Brecks.

For more details go to **www.VisitTheBroads.co.uk.**

Protecting the countryside

The Broads Authority wants everyone to enjoy their visit and to help keep the area a special place. You can do this by following the Countryside Code:

RESPECT EVERYONE
- Be considerate to those living in, working in and enjoying the countryside.
- Leave gates and property as you find them.
- Do not block access to gateways or driveways when parking.
- Be nice, say hello, share the space.
- Follow local signs and keep to marked paths unless wider access is available.

PROTECT THE NATURAL ENVIRONMENT
- Take your litter home – leave no trace of your visit.
- Take care with BBQs and do not light fires.
- Always keep your dogs under control and in sight.
- Dog poo – bag it and bin it in any public waste bin.
- Care for nature – do not cause damage or disturbance.

ENJOY THE OUTDOORS
- Check your route and local conditions.
- Plan your adventure – know what to expect and what you can do.
- Enjoy your visit, have fun, make a memory.

It's pretty easy to act responsibly when out walking. Simply take care not to disturb wild animals and sensitive habitats. Don't take things away like stones or wild flowers, and don't leave anything behind that you shouldn't.

Visit **www.broads-authority.gov.uk** for more information.

Walking tips & guidance

Safety

Walking will be safe and enjoyable provided a few simple rules are followed:

- Make sure you are fit enough to complete the walk.

- Always try to let others know where you intend to go.

- Take care around cliff edges and keep an eye on the tide.

- Wear sensible clothes and suitable footwear.

- Take ample water and food.

- Take a map or guide.

- Always allow plenty of time for the walk and be aware of when it will get dark.

- Walk at a steady pace. A zigzag route is usually a more comfortable way of negotiating a slope. Avoid going directly downhill as it's easier to lose control and may also cause erosion to the hillside.

- When walking on country roads, walk on the right-hand side facing the oncoming traffic, unless approaching a blind bend when you should cross over to the left so as to be seen from both directions.

- If the weather changes unexpectedly and visibility becomes poor, don't panic, but try to remember the last certain feature you passed and work out your route from that point on the map. Be sure of your route before continuing.

· Try not to dislodge stones on high edges or slopes.

Unfortunately, accidents can happen even on easy walks. If you're with someone who has an accident or can't continue, you should:

· Make sure the injured person is sheltered from further injury, although you should never move anyone with a head, neck or back injury.

· If you have a phone with a signal, call for help.

· If you can't get a signal and have to leave the injured person to go for help, try to leave a note saying what has happened and what first aid you have tried. Make sure you know the exact location so you can give accurate directions to the emergency services. When you get a signal or reach a telephone, call 999 and ask for the police, or the coastguard if you are on or near the water. The coastguard will call the other emergency services if needed.

Please take care on or near the water. Wear a life jacket, especially when getting on and off or mooring a boat. Canoeists should wear a buoyancy aid. Paddleboarders should wear a buoyancy aid and safety tether. Take care with dogs, too. There are Broads National Park yacht stations at Great Yarmouth, Reedham and Norwich, open during the main boating season, where staff can advise on all boating matters such as tides, preparing for bridges and crossing Breydon Water. The Broads National Park Rangers are also out on land and water all year to assist you if needed. Please don't drink and drive, sail or paddle on the water.

For full safety info go to **www.broads-authority.gov.uk/boating.**

Equipment

The equipment you will need depends on several factors, such as the type of activity planned, the time of year, and the weather likely to be encountered.

Clothing should be adequate for the day. In summer, remember sun screen, especially for your head and neck. Wear light woollen socks and lightweight boots or strong shoes. Even on hot days take an extra layer and waterproofs in your rucksack, just in case. Winter wear is a much more serious affair. Remember that once the body starts to lose heat, it becomes much less efficient. Jeans are particularly unsuitable for winter walking.

When considering waterproof clothing, it pays to buy the best you can afford. Make sure that the jacket is loose-fitting, windproof and has a generous hood. Waterproof overtrousers will not only offer protection against the rain, but they are also windproof. Clothing described as 'showerproof' will not keep you dry in heavy rain, and those made from rubberised or plastic materials can be heavy to carry and will trap moisture on the inside. Your rucksack should have wide, padded carrying straps for comfort.

It is important to wear boots that fit well or shoes with a good moulded sole – blisters can ruin any walk! Woollen socks are much more comfortable than any other fibre. The Broads is a wetland, so for a short Broads walk, at any time of the year, you may find wellington boots are preferable to shoes. Your clothes should be comfortable and not likely to catch on twigs and bushes.

It is important to carry a compass and a map or guide. A small first aid kit is also useful for treating cuts and other small injuries.

Finally, take a bottle of water and enough food to keep you going.

Bitterns frequent the reedbeds, feeding on amphibians, insects and fish

Public rights of way

Right of way means that anyone may walk freely on a defined footpath or ride a horse or bicycle along a public bridleway. In 1949, the National Parks and Access to the Countryside Act tidied up the law covering rights of way. Following public consultation, maps were drawn up by the Countryside Authorities of England and Wales to show all rights of way. Copies of these maps are available for public inspection and are invaluable when trying to resolve doubts over little-used footpaths. Once on the map, the right of way is irrefutable.

Any obstructions to a right of way should be reported to the local Highways Authority.

In England and Wales rights of way fall into three main categories:

- Public footpaths – for walkers only.

- Bridleways – for passage on foot, horseback or bicycle.

- Byways – for all the above and for motorised vehicles.

Free access to footpaths and bridleways does mean that certain guidelines should be followed as a courtesy to those who live and work in the area. For example, you should only sit down to picnic where it does not interfere with other walkers or the landowner. All gates must be kept closed to prevent stock from straying and dogs must be kept under close control – usually this is interpreted as meaning that they should be kept on a lead. Motorised vehicles must not be driven along a public footpath or bridleway without the landowner's consent.

A farmer may put a docile mature beef bull with a herd of cows or heifers in a field crossed by a public footpath. Beef bulls such as Herefords (usually brown / red in colour) are unlikely to be upset by passers-by but dairy bulls, like the black-and-white Friesian, can be dangerous by nature. It is, therefore, illegal for a farmer to let a dairy bull roam loose in a field open to public access.

The Countryside and Rights of Way Act 2000 allows access on foot to areas of legally defined 'open country' – mountain, moor, downland, heath and registered common land. It does not allow freedom to walk everywhere. It also increases protection for Sites of Special Scientific Interest, improves wildlife enforcement legislation and allows for better management of Areas of Outstanding Natural Beauty.

How to use this book

Each of the walks in this guide are set out in a similar way. They are all introduced with a simple locator map followed by a brief description of the area, its geography and history, and some notes on things you will encounter on your walk.

Near the start of each section there is a panel of information outlining the distance of the walk, the time it is expected to take and briefly describing the path conditions or the terrain you will encounter. A suggested starting point, along with grid reference is shown, as is the nearest postcode – although in rural locations postcodes can cover a large area and are therefore only a rough guide for sat nav users. It is always sensible to take a reference map with you, and the relevant OS Explorer map is also listed.

The major part of each section is taken up with a plan for each walk and detailed point by point description of our recommended route, along with navigational tips and points of interest.

Here is a description of the main symbols on the route maps:

Motorway	Railway station	30m Contour height (m)
Trunk/primary road	Bus station/stop	Walk route
Secondary road	Car park	Optional route
Tertiary road	Castle	Route instruction
Residential/unclassified road	Church	Open land
Service road	Lighthouse	Parks/sports grounds
Track	Interesting feature	Urban area
Pedestrian/bridleway/cycleway	Tourist information	Woodland
Footway/path	Cafe	Nature reserve
Railway	Pub	Wetland
Rivers/coast	Toilets	Lakes

WALK 1

Norwich Riverside,
River Wensum

*Norwich is the only English city with part of a
National Park in its midst. The stretch of the River
Wensum that flows through the city is part of the Broads.*

The river really brings the National Park and the countryside into
the city. Boats are on the water, trees grow beside it and Broads
wildlife is in and around it, so this walk is good for seeing wildlife
in the city, especially water birds, maybe even a kingfisher. There
are peregrine falcons nesting on the cathedral spire each year as
well. You may also catch a rare glimpse of an otter hunting near
the riverbank.

You'll also notice the contrasting architecture, from very old to
very new. As the country's second city in medieval times, this
sense of history really comes alive on the walk, with the city's
oldest bridge, Bishop Bridge, dating from 1340 and its newest, the
Jarrold Bridge, built in 2011.

Cow Tower (14th-century) is named after the surrounding
meadow, once known as Cowholme. The tower was built as an
addition to the defences already encircling medieval Norwich and
held both guns and a garrison to defend the approach to the city
across the River Wensum. Just over the river, in the 19th century,
Petch's Corner was the site of a wherry-building yard.

Stone for building Norwich Cathedral was transported by sea from
France, then up the rivers Yare and Wensum, and finally along a
canal (no longer in existence), which was constructed by monks.

Distance: 1.4 miles (2.3km)
Time: 1 hour
Terrain: Level paths, gates, ramp.
Start/Finish: Bishop Bridge
(TG240090); BA moorings:
Norwich Yacht Station
(charges apply)
Nearest Postcode: NR1 4AA
Map: OS Explorer OL40
The Broads

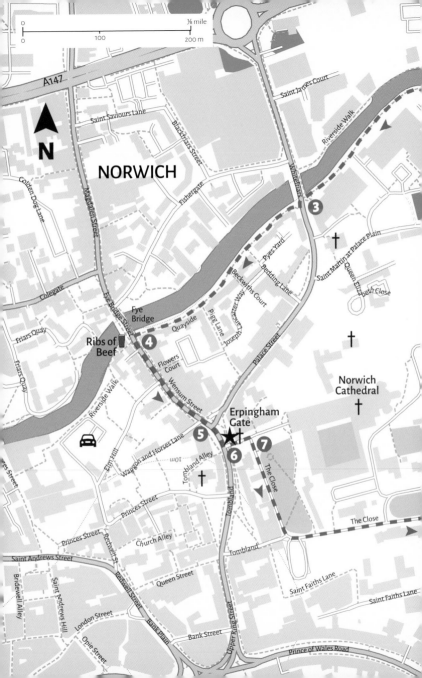

This journey was recreated for the cathedral's 900th anniversary. A huge piece of stone from Caen in Normandy stands at the main cathedral entrance, commemorating the link with Norwich Cathedral 1096–1996. Returning to the river, you'll see where the canal came in, at Pull's Ferry, a 15th-century watergate. It's named after one of the ferrymen, John Pull.

The railway station is close by for trains, buses and parking (opposite) and there's some short-stay on-street parking near the start of the walk. Please keep dogs on leads in the cathedral Close. Most facilities are nearby and as well as the cathedral, you can easily explore some of the other delights of Norwich from here. The Riverside Walk section closes at dusk.

1 Start from Bishop Bridge and with the river behind you, turn right past the Red Lion pub.

2 Follow the riverside footpath towards Cow Tower, past the Jarrold Bridge and on to Whitefriars Bridge.

3 Cross the road carefully at Whitefriars Bridge and follow the path opposite through to Quayside.

4 At Fye Bridge turn left along Wensum Street (opposite the Ribs of Beef pub) towards the cathedral.

5 Cross Palace Street carefully to reach the cathedral.

6 Enter the cathedral Close through the Erpingham Gate.

7 Turn right and then left to follow Ferry Lane down to Pull's Ferry, a flint building by the river. Norwich Yacht Station is on the far bank about 300 m down the river on your right.

8 Turn left to return to Bishop Bridge along the riverside path.

Cow Tower has stood on Norwich riverside for more than 600 years

WALK 2
Surlingham Church Marsh, River Yare

This is a short walk with lots of interest – there's even a (small) hill to go down and another in view.

With the River Yare, marshland and farmland, and lots of wildlife, this is a lovely country walk not far from Norwich. The walk follows footpaths through an RSPB nature reserve (open at all times).

Surlingham Church Marsh is made up of habitats including reedbeds, fens and pools, which attract marsh harriers, herons, kingfishers, water rails, and reed and sedge warblers in spring and summer. In winter the site attracts bitterns, gadwalls and shovelers. As well as the usual cattle, you may see Highland cattle on the fen areas. It's a peaceful and beautiful walk, close to the water. Please keep dogs on the paths, under control and on a lead where indicated.

The Ferry House pub is named after the ferry, which operated until 1939 – ferries were an important way of getting people and goods around in the Broads. You can visit St Mary's Church with its round tower and lovely churchyard, while 300 m away you can see the ruins of the 11th-century St Saviour's Church. Surlingham is on the Wherryman's Way if you want to extend your walk via lanes and paths to Wheatfen or Bramerton.

Distance: 1.9 miles (3.1 km)
Time: 1–1½ hours
Terrain: Mainly flat but uneven paths (which can be very wet, muddy and slippery), lane, track; slopes, gate, stiles.
Start/Finish: Church Lane, Surlingham (TG305064); BA moorings: Bramerton; moorings for customers at pub
Nearest Postcode: NR14 7DF
Map: OS Explorer OL40 The Broads

1 You can do this walk in either direction, starting from St Mary's Church, or if you'd like to visit the pub you can start from there (parking at both places). These directions go clockwise from the church. The route is waymarked and there are information panels by the church and at the bird hide. At the end of Church Lane take the path straight ahead with the cottage on your right. When you reach the bottom of the hill the path can be very muddy.

2 Continue straight ahead beside the dyke. When you reach the river enjoy the marsh views and turn right along the riverside path. This stretch is also often muddy and the river is very close so take care and supervise children.

3 Don't miss the large and comfortable bird hide, open to lovely views. The RSPB part of the walk is a Site of Special Scientific Interest.

4 When you reach a path on your right you can take a detour into the marsh or use it for a shorter loop back to the church. Otherwise, continue ahead along the riverside path.

5 At the pub, follow Ferry Road away from the river. In early spring look out for the bright yellow of marsh marigolds.

6 When you reach houses, take the first path on the right, go over the stiles and continue over grazing land, where there are often cows. Here's where you'll see that hill!

7 Don't be alarmed if you hear shooting on Thursdays and Sundays. The path goes alongside a gun club that operates then; there are warning signs.

8 You can take the field path to your left or continue on the main track, which then turns left. Where the track turns right, you can turn to your left and climb the short bank with steps to find the church ruins. Go back down to the path and continue straight ahead uphill to return to St Mary's Church.

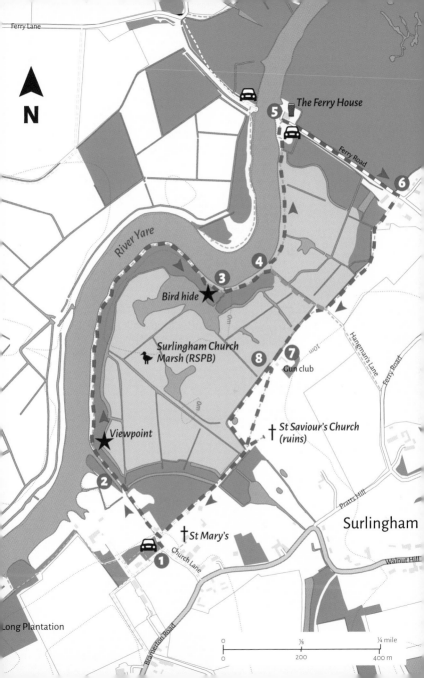

N

Ferry Lane

The Ferry House

5

Ferry Road

6

River Yare

4

3

Bird hide ★

Surlingham Church
Marsh (RSPB)

0m

8

7

Gun club

0m

10m

Hangman's Lane

Ferry Road

† St Saviour's Church
(ruins)

★ Viewpoint

2

Pratts Hill

Surlingham

† St Mary's

1

Church Lane

Walnut Hill

Bramerton Road

Long Plantation

0		⅛		¼ mile
0	200		400 m	

The Surlingham Church Marsh walk is a special mix of riverside, woodland and historical interest

WALK 3
Wheatfen, River Yare

'Let us remain a breathing space for the cure of souls.'

Ted Ellis, naturalist, writer and broadcaster, wrote these words about the East Anglian countryside. He lived at Wheaten for 40 years until 1986, and he was someone whose enthusiasm and care for the natural world naturally engaged and inspired others. He was the Keeper of Natural History at the Castle Museum in Norwich, discovering thousands of different species, many new to Norfolk and the UK.

Wheatfen is now a nature reserve and Site of Special Scientific Interest, but, above all, it's a place to feel the natural world living around you. The marshes are full of Broads wildlife, with a profusion of flowers in spring and summer. In spring, listen for the booming call of the bittern across the river. It's a great place to hear the cuckoo, too, or see a marsh harrier overhead. On a summer's day the dykes are full of dragonflies, damselflies, froglets and small fish. Swallowtail butterflies and Norfolk hawker dragonflies live here. The reserve is a typical freshwater wetland, and the paths take you close to the river and two small broads, as well as through mysterious woodland.

Our walk explores the nature reserve, but it's also on the Wherryman's Way long-distance route between Norwich and Great Yarmouth, so you can extend your walk to explore Surlingham or continue from Wheatfen towards Rockland St Mary. You can also stop off at the Yare Valley Farm Shop, just off The Covey, where you'll find local rapeseed oil, as well as Teles Patisserie, with a Portuguese flavour.

Distance: 2 miles (3 km)
Time: 1–2 hours
Terrain: 150 metres of easy
access boardwalk. Remaining
paths are uneven grass or
through woodland, often wet
and muddy, especially in winter.
Start/Finish: Wheatfen, The
Covey, Surlingham (TG324056);
BA moorings: Rockland St Mary
Nearest Postcode: NR14 7AL
Map: OS Explorer OL40
The Broads

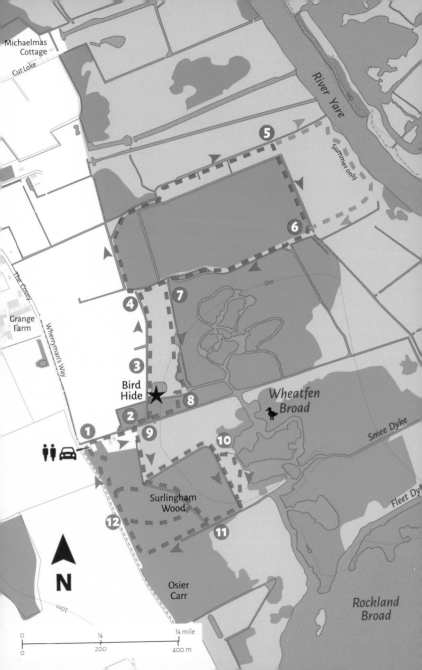

Michaelmas Cottage

Cut Loke

River Yare

Summer only

5

6

7

The Covey

Grange Farm

Wherryman's Way

4

3

Bird Hide ★ 8

2

1

9

10

Wheatfen Broad

Smee Dyke

0m

Surlingham Wood

11

12

Fleet Dyke

Osier Carr

Rockland Broad

10m

N

0   ⅛   ¼ mile
0   200   400 m

1 The reserve is open daily from sunrise to sunset, with an additional, often very wet path open in summer. Occasionally, during heavy rain or big winter tides, the reserve is closed due to flooding. At the car park you'll find the Warden's office with free reserve maps available outside; paths are also waymarked. There is a car park alighting point and toilet for disabled visitors. Assistance dogs are welcome on a lead. From the car park, head through the gateway on the path going past the cottage.

2 When you reach the dyke, turn left to the boardwalk and left again at the junction.

3 A thatched bird hide by the boardwalk acts as an information point, offering details of the reserve's history, management and rare species. One of the special features of Wheatfen is that you can lose yourself in another, more peaceful world, but you are unlikely to actually get lost. Leave the hide and turn right.

4 Continue to the junction of paths and turn left. Follow the path towards the river.

5 Turn right on the all-year path or continue to the river and then turn right on the summer path, which eventually joins the main path.

6 Continue on the main path.

7 & **8** Follow the paths back towards the head of the dyke near the start of the walk.

9 When you reach it, go straight ahead towards Surlingham Wood (with the cottage on your right).

10, **11** & **12** Several paths will take you through the wood and back to the car park, but don't miss out the detour to Wheatfen Broad.

Wheatfen, River Yare | Broads   33

WALK 4
Hardley, River Chet

This is a walk for any time of the year, where you can enjoy big skies and wildlife, peace and quiet, and get a sense of hundreds of years of history around you.

From Hardley Staithe, the local name for a mooring place, walking east along the River Yare, you'll reach Hardley Cross. The original wooden cross was erected in 1543, marking the ancient boundary of the legal powers of the City of Norwich and the Borough of Great Yarmouth. For hundreds of years officials sailed here for an annual ceremony to settle disputes relating to trade on the River Yare. The present stone cross is thought to date from 1676.

Look for a variety of wildlife including otters, deer, geese, ducks, swans, marsh harriers, kestrels, barn owls, reed buntings and yellowhammers, as well as swallows in the summer. There's plenty of Norfolk reed along the waterways. Livestock graze in the surrounding fields.

You'll also see Hardley Hall and the lovely Hardley Church. This round-tower church is mainly 14th-15th century and contains medieval wall paintings.

There are great views of Hardley Mill and Cantley sugar factory along the River Yare. The sugar beet processing plant, which opened in 1912, is the last vestige of trade on the Broads. Sugar beet was delivered by water and then removed by water in the form of refined sugar. The factory's last use of water transport was employment of the Blackheath, which brought oil from Great Yarmouth to Cantley until the 2000s.

Distance: 3.6 miles (5.8 km)
Time: 1½ hours
Terrain: Fairly flat route on mostly grass paths and lanes; river path can be uneven; gates. Walk is exposed in parts and it can be windy.
Start/Finish: Hardley Staithe, Hardley Staithe Road, Hardley (TG388011); BA moorings: Hardley Cross
Nearest Postcode: NR14 6BU
Map: OS Explorer OL40 The Broads

Back at the staithe, if you walk west along the River Yare you'll reach Hardley Mill. This mill dates from 1874 and drained the adjoining marshes. It powered a turbine, capable of raising 12 tons of water per minute. It operated until around 1950, when it was damaged and replaced by an electric pump. The mill has recently been restored to full working order and you may even see the sails turning – there is also a vistor centre.

Hardley is close to the little market town of Loddon, adjoined by Chedgrave. They are on either side of the River Chet – you'll find old churches, shops, pubs, cafes and toilets.

1 Start from the staithe, where parking is available, or from Hardley Cross moorings. At Hardley Staithe, facing down Hardley Dyke, follow the right-hand bank. When you reach the River Yare continue to the right along the bank.

2 At Hardley Cross, follow the River Chet to the right.

3 Turn right on the track leading towards Hardley Hall. Continue until you reach a lane.

4 Turn right along Hardley Hall Lane towards the church.

5 Near the church, turn right along Hardley Staithe Road and continue back to the staithe.

Optional: You can extend this walk by about a mile and a half by heading upsteam on the Yare to visit Hardley Mill, one of the most active drainage windmills in the region.

6 To continue the walk by going to Hardley Mill, facing along the dyke take the left-hand bank and then turn left along the River Yare.

7 Retrace your steps back to Hardley Staithe.

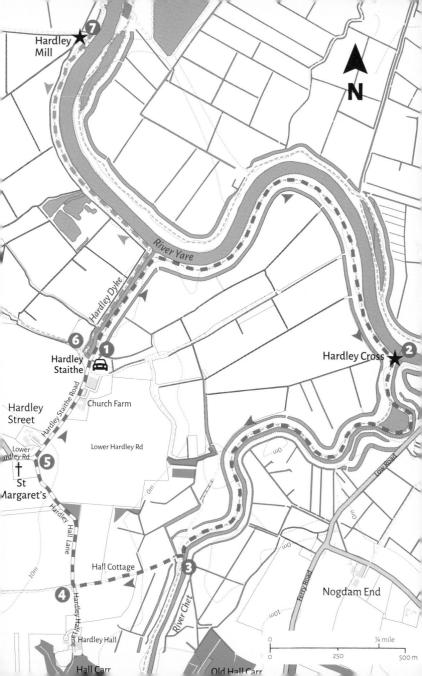

N

Hardley Mill ★ 7

River Yare

Hardley Dyke

Hardley Cross ★ 2

6
1 🚗
Hardley Staithe

Church Farm

Hardley Street

Hardley Staithe Road

Lower Hardley Rd

Lower Hardley Rd

5

† St Margaret's

0m

0m

0m

River Chet

Low Road

Ferry Road

Hardley Hall Lane

Hall Cottage

3

Nogdam End

10m

4

Hardley Hall Lane

Hardley Hall

10m

Hall Carr

Old Hall Carr

| 0 | | ¼ mile |
| 0 | 250 | 500 m |

WALK 5

Reedham, River Yare

Here's a walk to remind you of other ways of getting around the Broads – by train and by ferry. If you are travelling by train, please check train timetables carefully.

Reedham is on the Wherry Lines, running from Norwich to Great Yarmouth and Lowestoft, and the ferry goes across the Yare to the Loddon and Chedgrave area. The railway swing bridge and the chain ferry are very distinctive Broads features. The ferry is one of the few remaining in the Broads and even takes vehicles. There has been a crossing at Reedham since the early 17th century and the original ferry's main users were horse-drawn vehicles. In 1949 the ferry was still hand-wound across the river, but early in 1950 it became motorised.

Enjoy the quiet and the extensive views over the marshes, with plenty of wild flowers to see and opportunities for bird watching. While in Reedham you could also visit the church, and the village has refreshments, a shop and toilets.

A good addition to the walk is to follow the Wherryman's Way signs (from just by the Ship Inn, going along Holly Farm Road) towards Polkey's Mill along the riverbank. The site of the group of mill buildings is also known as the Seven Mile Site, after the distance by river to Great Yarmouth. The site isn't open on a regular basis but the walk gives more wonderful views of the marshes. From Reedham, it's about 45 minutes each way; please keep dogs on leads.

Distance: 3.8 miles (6.1 km)
Time: 2 hours
Terrain: Footpaths, lanes, gates and steps.
Start/Finish: Reedham Quay, Reedham
(TG419017); BA moorings: Reedham Quay
Nearest Postcode: NR13 3TE
Map: OS Explorer OL40 The Broads

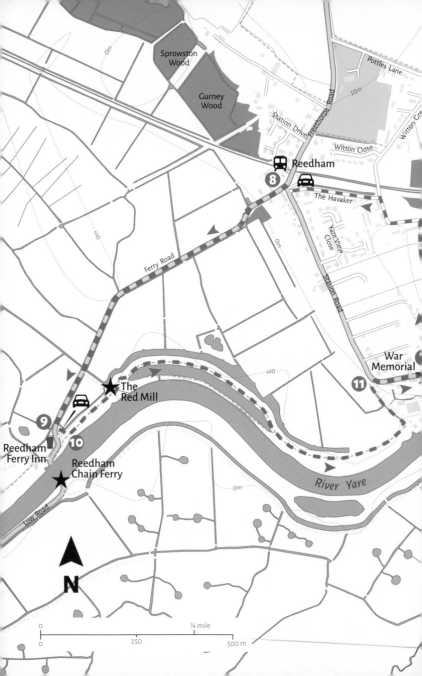

Sprowston
Wood

Gurney
Wood

Pottles Lane

Station Drive

Freethorpe Road

Witton Green

Witton Close

🚃 Reedham

8

The Havaker

Ferry Road

Yare View Close

Station Road

0m

War
Memorial

11

★ The
Red Mill

9

10

Reedham Ferry Inn

Reedham
Chain Ferry

★

River Yare

Low Road

0m

N

0		¼ mile
0	250	500 m

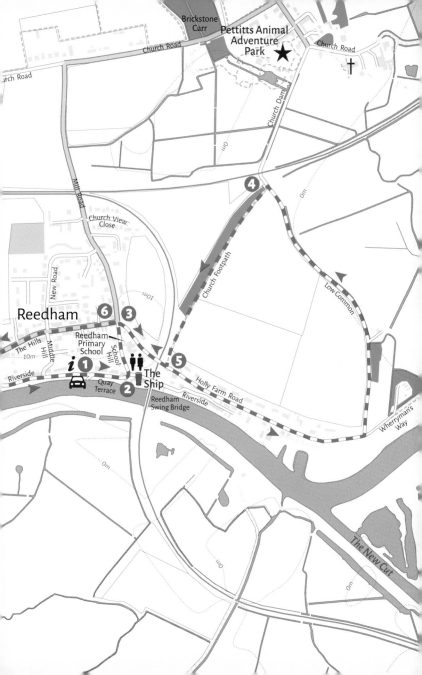

1 From the quay (parking available), with your back to the river, turn right towards the bridge.

2 Just before the bridge, the road goes past The Ship and turns left uphill (School Hill), past the public toilets and towards Reedham School.

3 After the school, turn sharp right into Holly Farm Road. Follow the road to a junction of paths and a road. Follow the tarmac road, Low Common, going left.

4 Just before the level crossing turn sharp left down a footpath. This will bring you out at the bridge over the railway on Holly Farm Road.

5 Turn right along the road back to the junction by the school.

6 Cross the road to The Hills, almost opposite Holly Farm Road. This road runs parallel to Reedham Quay but is considerably higher.

7 Near the war memorial take a right turn up the hill on a footpath that goes towards the station. At the end of the path turn left, then right, then left on to Witton Green and The Havaker.

8 Approaching the station, turn left down Ferry Road.

9 On reaching Reedham Ferry Inn go through the car park, then climb the steps to get to the riverbank.

10 Turn left and follow the footpath past the Red Mill. The footpath continues to the edge of Reedham, where you go left down another set of steps and follow the field edge.

11 When the path emerges on to Station Road go right towards the war memorial and then bear right to go down Riverside back to the quay.

Polkey's Mill is about 2½ miles east of Reedham, follow the Wherryman's Way

WALK 6

Halvergate Marshes and Berney Arms, River Yare

The grazing marshes around the River Yare are often referred to as Halvergate Marshes, although in fact there are many other areas of marsh here associated with other villages.

It's a place to enjoy the wide horizons of the Broads and a sense of wildness and remoteness, but please take care. It's a great place to visit by train (various combinations of walking and train travel are possible), but check timetables very carefully in advance. Take adequate supplies of food and water, bearing in mind you could be delayed. It's very exposed to the elements, with no shelter, so take appropriate protection for sun, wind, cold and rain. There are no facilities or services on the walk after you leave Great Yarmouth. Make sure also that you won't be walking in the dark. The area can be explored by other footpaths from villages, or from the moorings, but there are no proper roads.

The grazing marshes here epitomise the marshland landscape of the Broads – vast panoramic views, winding waterways, wide-open skies and a sense of space. Cows may walk up on to the top of the dyke at times. The landscape is set with drainage mills, many of which are being restored. There's a sense of being connected to nature and history – you can picture what life was like on the marshes a century ago as the area seems relatively unchanged. You'll see where the rivers Yare and Waveney meet, with Burgh Castle visible across them.

Look out for birds of prey such as marsh harriers, and mammals including Chinese water deer and hares. Spring and summer bring

Distance: 5.5 miles (8.9 km)
Time: 2½–3 hours
Terrain: Mostly flat ground; grass surfaces or tracks can be uneven, with holes; gates, kissing gates, stiles and steps.
Start/Finish: Great Yarmouth Railway Station, Acle New Road, Great Yarmouth (TG520081); BA moorings: Great Yarmouth Yacht Station (charges apply), Berney Arms; the distance and time given are one-way, Berney Arms to Great Yarmouth, with the outward journey by train
Nearest Postcode: NR30 1SD
Map: OS Explorer OL40 The Broads

many butterflies and dragonflies. The network of ditches and dykes is full of wildlife, and fringed with grasses and wild flowers. Egrets, goldfinches and wagtails are among the many birds to see here. Berney Marshes and Breydon Water is an RSPB nature reserve and in the winter there can be up to 100,000 waders and wildfowl, including lapwings, wigeons, pink-footed geese and golden plovers.

Berney Arms Station is one of the smallest and most remote in the country. You can also make use of the stations at Norwich and Reedham to combine train travel with walking sections of the Wherryman's Way, which runs between Norwich and Great Yarmouth. Trading wherries used this route as well as others throughout the Broads, carrying cargoes of stone, wood, reed, even ice, in fact pretty much any load that needed to be transported.

1 Berney Arms Station is a request stop. To leave the train here, inform the conductor or driver in good time. The platform is not long enough to take the whole train so listen carefully to instructions. (To board the train at this station, as the train approaches, give a clear hand signal to the driver, but keep well back from the track.) Take great care crossing the railway track.

2 From the station, take the Weavers' Way path going straight ahead across the marshes towards the tall Berney Arms Mill.

3 At the mill, go through the gate and up the steps on the right.

4 Turn left along the riverbank. The Weavers' Way joins the Wherryman's Way and the path will take you back to Great Yarmouth, along the river, skirting Breydon Water. Keep going!

5 Approaching Great Yarmouth, the path goes under a bridge and then alongside a supermarket car park to take you back to the station.

WALK 7

Bungay, River Waveney

This route combines a leafy woodland walk with open views and a visit to historic Bungay.

The Waveney forms the border between Norfolk and Suffolk and the market town of Bungay is tucked into a wide meander. You're never far from the river in Bungay, where you can explore the delights of Falcon Meadow or Outney Common. On this walk, in warm summer weather, the water attracts great clouds of wonderful damselflies and you may hear a cuckoo near the quarry.

In the town, look out for the 17th-century Butter Cross in the centre of the Market Place – a weekly market still takes place around the Butter Cross each Thursday. You can also see St Mary's Church and the Benedictine priory ruins that lie behind it.

Cross St Mary's Street by the Butter Cross and go through the passageway to find the castle ruins and lots of information about the medieval Bigods. Nowadays you can even buy locally-made Baron Bigod cheese, while Bigod's Kitchen cafe guards the entrance to the site at Castle Orchard.

And finally, beware of Shuck or Shock – the black dog of Bungay, who terrorised the church congregation on Sunday 4 August in 1577.

Distance: 5.5 miles (8.9 km)
Time: 2½ hours
Terrain: Uneven ground, hills, muddy or slippery conditions; kissing gate and stiles.
Start/Finish: Bigod's Castle, Castle Street, Bungay (TM335896)
Nearest Postcode: NR35 1AE
Map: OS Explorer OL40 The Broads

1 The walk starts from the castle in the centre of Bungay, where car parks, refreshments, shops and toilets are available. With your back to the castle take the footpath to your right, signposted Castle Inn. The footpath opens up into the Castle Inn courtyard before reaching Earsham Street.

2 Turn left on Earsham Street and, taking care of traffic, head out of Bungay, keeping on the footpath on the right. Go over the first bridge and on towards the second bridge.

3 At the start of the second bridge, cross the road and take the path, keeping the waterway on your right. Continue until you see a footbridge across the waterway.

4 Cross the footbridge and follow the track into the village of Earsham, past some cottages and All Saints' Church, until you reach Lodge Cottage on the right.

5 In between Lodge Cottage and number 20 follow the footpath signposted Angles Way Beccles. This footpath takes you through the village, then into Station Road until you reach the A143. Take care here to cross the busy road into Hall Road.

6 Follow Hall Road and then turn right to follow Bath Hills Road. You'll pass an old water-filled quarry on the right before reaching the main quarry.

7 At Valley Farm and Cottage keep walking ahead along the track. After walking through a wooden gate (which may be locked open) bear left along the track with hedges on either side and continue into woods. Notice the contour lines on the map showing the height above sea level – this is one of the highest points in the Broads.

8 Go through the gate and walk up the drive ahead.

9 At the top of the hill near The Wood House, bear right, signposted Bigod's Way Bungay 2 miles. Continue through the woods, with fields to your left, before descending towards a driveway. Cross the driveway and go through the gate into woods.

10 Take the first footpath on the right to return to Bungay over the common. However, this route can be liable to flooding. For an alternative route, take the first footpath on the left, which takes you to the village of Ditchingham, with a restaurant on the left. Turn right and take care crossing the A143. There's a roundabout and you'll see the old maltings buildings. Follow Ditchingham Dam into the centre of Bungay and back to the start.

WALK 8
Beccles and Geldeston, River Waveney

This is a Norfolk and Suffolk walk – the north bank of the Waveney is in Norfolk, while the southern part of the walk is in Suffolk, on the Angles Way.

It's a great walk and mostly very peaceful. You'll see a mixture of town, village and country. Some of the marshes on this walk can be liable to flooding and can become impassable in the winter.

There's a car park off Fen Lane, toilets at The Quay, and Beccles has a railway station and plenty of buses. Along the riverbank there are views of Beccles and the houses and gardens coming down to the river. Near the Locks Inn, on a clear day as you look far to the left, you should be able to see the Bell Tower of St Michael's Church at Beccles dominating the skyline.

The river was improved for navigation, and three locks were built at Geldeston, Ellingham and Wainford to extend navigation as far as Bungay. Construction of the cut from the river (Geldeston Dyke) allowed the commercial development of the village, and from the early 18th century its prosperity and local importance grew. Two large maltings were built, one at the staithe, the other, including a brewery, behind the Wherry Inn. There is still a boatyard at the staithe and the dyke provides access to the river for leisure craft.

As well as the numerous shops and places to eat in Beccles, Dunburgh Farm at Geldeston is an ideal refreshment stop.

Distance: 7 miles (11.3 km)
Time: 2½ hours
Terrain: Paths, tracks, lanes, roads. Can be muddy. Stiles, gates and steps.
Start/Finish: Yacht Station, The Quay, Fen Lane, Beccles (TM421911); BA moorings: Beccles and Geldeston
Nearest Postcode: NR34 9BH
Map: OS Explorer OL40 The Broads

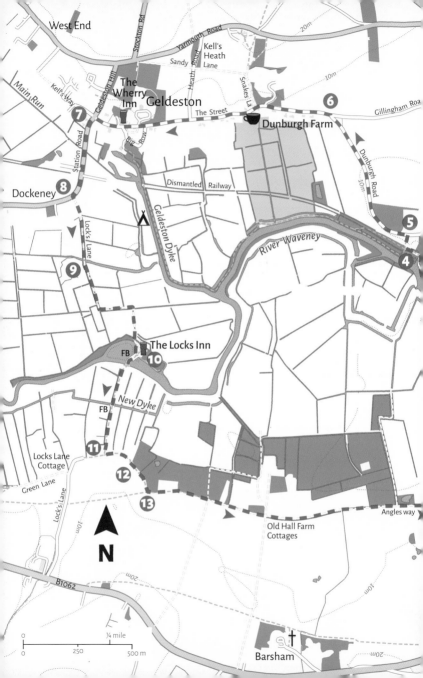

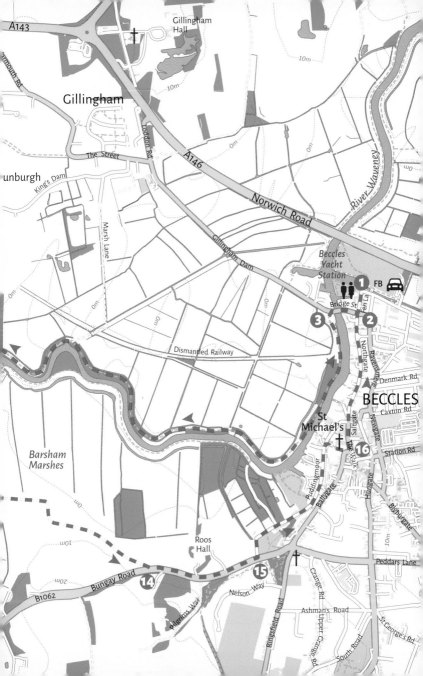

1 With the dyke behind you and the toilets to the right, go straight ahead along Fen Lane towards the town centre.

2 At the crossroads turn right towards the road bridge, following the footpath on the right and over the bridge.

3 Once over the river, cross the road and take the footpath going through a yard and along the riverbank.

4 The path turns slightly inland towards an elevated house amongst the trees, overlooking the river. At the footpath junction turn right and head uphill (with steps) until you reach Dunburgh Road.

5 Turn left along this lane and continue until you reach a busier road, The Street, heading towards Geldeston.

6 Turn left and follow the road into Geldeston.

7 Just after the Wherry Inn the road comes to a junction. Turn left down Station Road where you will see the distinctive old station house on the right.

8 Shortly after crossing the old railway line and just as the road curves to the right, you'll see a track to the left signposted Locks Inn.

9 Follow the track to the Locks Inn.

10 From the Locks Inn, head to the right over two bridges over the river and across the marsh, and over a further wooden bridge, towards a gate.

11 Once through the gate, turn left along the track, towards a further gate on the right, which gives access to a field.

12 Go through the gate and follow the field edge to the next gate.

13 Turn left at the gate and keep going straight ahead over a stile. Follow the field edge past cottages on the right, then keep going straight ahead until you reach cottages by the main Bungay to Beccles road (B1062).

14 Turn left and walk on the grass verge, passing Elizabethan Roos Hall on your left, until you reach a lane called Puddingmoor on your left.

15 Turn down Puddingmoor and continue until you reach the fourth set of steps on your right, immediately below the church. Go up the steps to St Michael's Church and the Bell Tower.

16 Turn left and follow The Walk, Saltgate and Northgate back to the yacht station.

WALK 9

Beccles Marsh Trail, River Waveney

This walk takes in a stretch of the Angles Way, with plenty of opportunities for big sky views across the marshes.

Transport and routes are a theme. Close to the sailing club there's the site of an Iron Age causeway, with evidence of later Roman additions. Causeways constructed of faggots or gravel were maintained to provide access for wheeled carts. Later on, you'll come to the remains of an old railway bridge, part of the Waveney Valley line, which ran from Beccles to the East Coast main line.

The dyke systems on the marshes originate from medieval times and the Worlingham Wall is a medieval flood defence that divided Beccles Marshes from Worlingham Marshes. These flood walls divided the common marshes of each parish, where parishioners had the right to graze their animals. The marshes are still grazed by cattle today and are criss-crossed by small dykes. There are occasional organised game shoots on the marshes.

In spring coots, moorhens and swans nest in the dykes. You may hear lapwings, and the first flowers appear, usually yellow, the most attractive colour for insects. The first butterfly, the brimstone, is yellow too. Early summer brings cuckoo calls. Summer flowers include marigolds, mallow and purple loosestrife, and you may even see the blue flash of a kingfisher. Late summer brings butterflies such as peacocks, painted ladies, red admirals and commas, as well as dragonflies and damselflies. In autumn the oak leaves are changing colour and in winter ducks and geese inhabit the wet fields. Birds of prey such as kestrels, marsh harriers, buzzards and owls hover, looking for small mammals.

Distance: 4.7 miles (7.6 km)
Time: 2½ hours
Terrain: Some paths can be uneven, wet, muddy, slippery, narrow and overgrown. Very high tides can cause flooding.
Start/Finish: Yacht Station, The Quay, Fen Lane, Beccles (TM421911); BA moorings: Beccles, by A146 bridge
Nearest Postcode: NR34 9BH
Map: OS Explorer OL40 The Broads

1 The route starts at the yacht station and the main car park is off Fen Lane. You can also start from the BA Beccles moorings or from the car park for disabled visitors (near the A146 roundabout), from where there's a short easy access route. From the yacht station turn left and cross the footbridge, then turn left towards the river, walking along the dyke.

2 At the river turn right and walk under the A146 bridge and on past the Beccles Amateur Sailing Club and the site of the causeway.

3 Continue along the raised grassy footpath, which now runs along the dyke separating the Waveney from the marsh. You'll pass the remains of the river bridge.

4 About halfway round the walk, turn right off the Angles Way on to a waymarked path across the marshes.

5 Follow this path, crossing a footbridge, until you reach a gate and track.

6 Walk along the track and at the T-junction turn left. Keep to the track, which bears right, until you reach some farm buildings and a concrete area.

7 Turn left down the side of the farm buildings (stables) – look out for horses, which can canter up and down the tracks.

8 At the end of the track, go through the gate to join another track. You'll pass fishing lakes on your right.

9 At the end of the track bear right, passing allotments on your right.

10 After passing the car park for disabled visitors on your left, take the ramp up on to the easy access path, which follows the A146 back to the river.

11 At the river turn left to retrace your steps to the yacht station.

Beccles Marsh Trail, River Waveney | Broads

There are many opportunities for sailing on the River Waveney

WALK 10

Carlton Marshes, River Waveney

One of the greatest impressions is that of space —
somewhere else to enjoy the East Anglian big skies.

This is a great place for a walk if you are a wildlife watcher, but great if you're a child who just wants to play too. There are six marked viewing points, three of which are bird hides, so you may want to allow extra time for a stop at these, or indeed for a stop at the playground. Wheelchair users and pushchairs can use a firm path around part of the marsh, with easy access gates.

Carlton Marshes is now a huge wetland reserve with many bird species coming and going according to the season. During 2020 it was totally transformed when Suffolk Wildlife Trust's ambitious plans to acquire and adapt farmland to create a thousand-acre reserve for wildlife and people came to fruition. There are breeding waders such as avocet, lapwing and redshank, as well as other Broads species such as marsh harrier, fen raft spider, water vole and otter. The reserve is now also one of the most diverse sites in the UK for dragonflies, with 28 species recorded. Look out too for deer, stoats, hares – and cattle grazing.

On the Peto's Marsh walk you'll also see the mooring for the foot ferry if you'd like to go over from Suffolk to the Norfolk side of the river. The marsh is named after Sir Samuel Morton Peto, the Victorian engineer and railway pioneer, who lived at nearby Somerleyton Hall. If you're on a boat, the BA Dutch Tea Gardens moorings on the other side of Oulton Dyke give access to Oulton Marshes (sadly the tea gardens are long gone).

Distance: Share Marsh 1.8 miles (2.9 km), Peto's Marsh 3.5 miles (5.6 km)

Time: 1 hour for Share Marsh, 2 hours for Peto's Marsh

Terrain: Some paths suitable for wheelchair users. Parts of this reserve are accessible by mobility scooter. Some paths can be muddy in winter.

Start/Finish: Carlton Marshes, Burnt Hill Lane, Carlton Colville (TM508919); BA moorings: Peto's Marsh; you can walk from Oulton Broad South and North railway stations (20 and 30 minutes)

Nearest Postcode: NR33 8HU

Map: OS Explorer OL40 The Broads

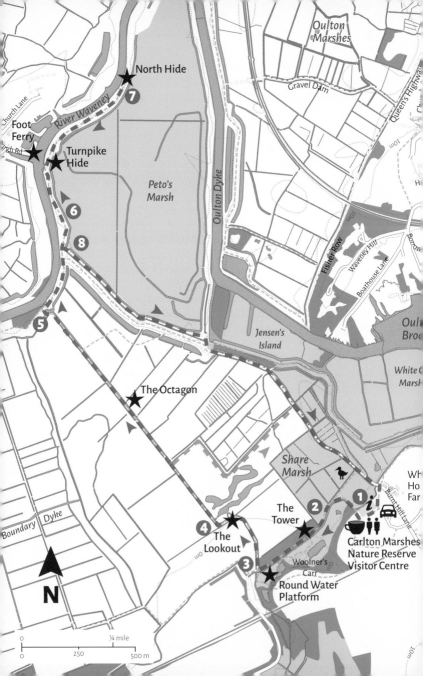

Oulton Marshes

Gravel Dam

Queen's Highway

North Hide

7

Church Lane

River Waveney

Foot Ferry

High Rd

Turnpike Hide

6

8

Peto's Marsh

Oulton Dyke

Fisher Row

Waveney Hill

Boathouse Lane

Barr

5

Jensen's Island

Oulton Brook

White Marsh

The Octagon

Share Marsh

1

Carlton Marshes Nature Reserve Visitor Centre

Burnt Hill Lane

Wh Ho Far

2

The Tower

4

The Lookout

3

Woolner's Carr

Round Water Platform

Boundary Dyke

N

¼ mile

0   250   500 m

1 The walk starts from the visitor centre. Dogs on leads are welcome.

2 The path is waymarked from the visitor centre, so follow it to the west keeping the waterway to your left. The path bends to the right after about 100 m and then bears left before reaching a junction. Keep to the left and stay on the path for another 200 m.

3 At this point there is a little bridge over the waterway to the left. Don't take the bridge but instead stay on the right-hand side of the waterway and turn right on to the well-trodden path alongside the marshy fields.

4 The path takes about 300 m to make a large bend to the left (in several small, straight sections). Eventually it comes to a sharp 90-degree turn to the right where you can see great views over the marshes. Start along the very straight path heading north-west.

Optional: After about 300 m the Share Marsh waymarked path heads off to the right. This shorter walk follows a zigzag path across the marsh before joining the longer route on its return to the visitor centre.

If you are taking in the longer Peto's Marsh walk, continue past the Share Marsh turn-off and stay on the straight path for almost a mile – until you reach the River Waveney.

5 At the river turn to the right to follow the path along the riverside as it heads north. After about 200 m you reach a junction. The path on the right goes back to the visitor centre but for now continue along the side of the river.

6 Peto's Marsh is now on the right, but stay on the riverside path and you will soon come to two bird hides (Turnpike Hide and North Hide). These offer great opportunities to sit and watch the wildlife.

7 From North Hide turn and retrace your route until you see the path on the left (mentioned at point 5).

8 This time take the path – to the left as it is now – and follow it and the waterway back to the visitor centre.

WALK 11
Herringfleet Hills, River Waveney

Herringfleet is one of the last of the smock mills in the Broads and dates from 1820.

This is a short walk, but one with lots of variety. You can also start the walk from either of the moorings, and Duke's Head customers can start from there. The walk is accessible from Somerleyton Station, with a little path to the boatyard and then to the walk route.

Herringfleet Hills is an open access area of grass heath surrounded by bracken, low scrub and woodland. Dogs are welcome on a lead but take care with nesting birds. Listen for songbirds such as whitethroats, willow warblers and yellowhammers in spring and summer. Look out for marsh harriers over the marshes and wading birds such as snipe, lapwings and redshanks. The area is good for butterflies, grass snakes and common lizards. The open expanse at Herringfleet Hills contrasts with the woods and riverside paths. The grazing marshes and reedbeds are very atmospheric in all weathers, with big sky views.

The mill is grade II listed, an octagonal building with three storeys, clad in tarred weatherboards, with a boat-shaped cap and external scoop wheel. It was built by millwright Robert Barnes of Great Yarmouth and was worked by a marshman until 1956. Like many Broads mills, it's part of the Broads Authority's Water, Mills & Marshes restoration scheme.

Distance: 1.8 miles (2.9 km)
Time: 1 hour
Terrain: Mainly level, steep slope from car park, gates, steps; paths can be muddy in wet weather, especially in winter.
Start/Finish: Herringfleet Hills car park, St Olaves Road (TM469982); BA moorings: Herringfleet and Somerleyton
Nearest Postcode: NR32 5QU
Map: OS Explorer OL40 The Broads

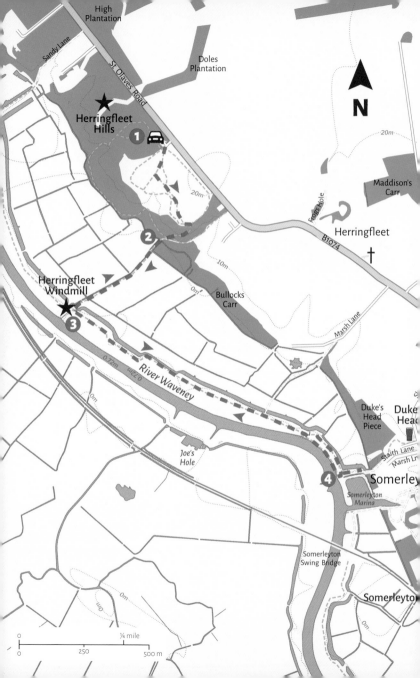

Somerleyton Bridge was built in 1905 to take the railway over the River Waveney and opens to allow larger boats to pass through. It was originally designed to operate without the technology available today.

Somerleyton village, and Somerleyton Hall and Gardens are close by. The gardens include a wonderful yew hedge maze, planted in 1846, in which to lose yourself. The surrounding parkland is being rewilded with cattle, wild ponies and deer roaming freely.

1 From the car park (set back from the road) pass through the gate and go straight ahead following a track. This goes slightly right before going quite steeply downhill through woods.

2 At the bottom of the hill bear left along a path until you see a metal gate on the right. Go through the gate and ahead to the mill. At the mill, cross the dyke on the bridge and go up the steps to the top of the bank.

3 Turn left and continue on this path to Somerleyton moorings.

4 Retrace your steps, turning right at the mill, to return to the start.

5 Alternatively, when you reach Herringfleet Hills, take the circular route. As it's an open access area, you can enjoy the right to some roaming. So long as you are heading up you'll reach the car park and St Olaves Road. (If you go down you'll be heading back to the river.)

Dating from 1820, Herringfleet Mill is one of the last wooden pumping mills on the Broads, still in working order

WALK 12
Burgh Castle, River Waveney

Burgh Castle is a place of contrasts, the massive flint ruins beside you and the soft landscape of Halvergate Marshes as you look out over what used to be the Great Estuary.

Burgh Castle, or Gariannonum, is the remains of a third-century Roman fort standing near the confluence of the rivers Waveney and Yare before they flow into Breydon Water, the remains of that estuary. The castle was built as one of the Saxon Shore forts to defend the coast from Saxon raiders. Soldiers at Burgh Castle were part of the Roman army. By about 900 a long bar of sand and shingle had formed across the mouth of the Great Estuary, the site of the future Great Yarmouth. Three of the castle walls remain – the fourth has disappeared into the Waveney. This Norfolk Archaeological Trust site is open dawn to dusk; the car park closes at 18:00. Dogs on leads are welcome.

Set in the wonderful view over the marshes is Berney Arms Mill, one of the tallest drainage mills in the country. Back in the 1980s, this huge area of marshes could have disappeared. Saving Halvergate grazing marshes from deep drainage for arable crops was a cause that drew national support. Out of it, the Broads Authority developed the Broads Grazing Marsh Conservation Scheme, forerunner of the national Environmentally Sensitive Areas scheme, which continued into the 2000s.

Distance: 1.4 miles (2.3 km)
Time: 1–1½ hours
Terrain: Wheelchair access, with wide kissing gates, from the car park and around the fortifications, easy slope up to the fort. Some other paths can be muddy. Mainly very flat. Paths, boardwalks, grass, stiles.
Start/Finish: Burgh Castle, Butt Lane, Burgh Castle (TG479048); moorings: Burgh Castle
Nearest Postcode: NR31 9QQ
Map: OS Explorer OL40 The Broads

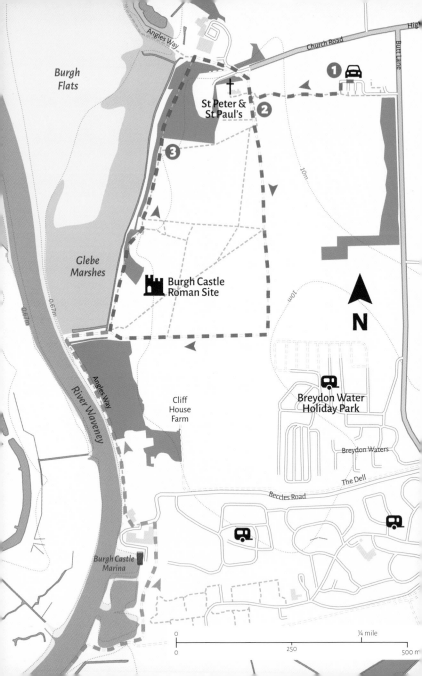

The reedbeds below the fort are home to bearded tits, reed and sedge warblers, water rails and yellow wagtails. On the tidal mudflats you can see a variety of wildfowl and waders. Look out too for egrets, shelduck, barn owls and gulls. There are also large wild flower meadows. Marsh and hen harriers frequent the area in winter.

You can also visit the medieval round-tower church of St Peter and St Paul, with lovely stained glass.

It's all together a peaceful place, full of history, with space for you to roam. If you want to plan some longer walks, the Angles Way long-distance footpath runs through the site and continues to Great Yarmouth, where it links up with the Weavers' Way and the Wherryman's Way.

1 From the car park (or the church) follow the marked path.

Optional: If you are starting from the moorings, a signed path, not accessible to wheelchair users, also leads to the fort.

2 Follow the marked paths around and into the fortifications.

3 Return to your starting point.

The remains of a Roman fort at Burgh Castle date back to the third century

WALK 13

Coltishall and Horstead, River Bure

A village and river walk — you could also start this walk from Wroxham or Aylsham, taking the narrow-gauge Bure Valley Railway to Coltishall.

The walk starts with a pleasant stroll along Coltishall Common and through the attractive village (with shops and places to eat). Coltishall was home to boatbuilding from the early 1800s and Allen's boatyard was in Anchor Street – the last trading wherry, Ella, was built here in 1912. Wherries were Broads cargo boats, with a shallow draught and a huge single sail. The river was navigable as far as Horstead Mill and was canalised to Aylsham using locks.

Approaching Horstead Mill you'll see the site of a lock keeper's cottage and an old beech hedge. You can have a wander here around the remains of the 18th-century water mill and its mill-pool – look out for grey wagtails.

Once you leave the villages behind, you're into the Norfolk countryside, including long stretches of river overlooking meadows, very quiet and peaceful. Listen for skylarks in the meadows. There are plenty of contrasting habitats along the walk with fen and woodland as well. The riverside is a good habitat for kingfishers and depending on the time of year, there are lots of wild flowers, including flag iris, periwinkle, cranesbill, mallow and speedwell. In summer the walk is alive with banded demoiselle damselflies, dragonflies, and orange-tip and red admiral butterflies.

Distance: 6.5 miles (10.5 km)
Time: 3–3½ hours
Terrain: Paths can be muddy and uneven. Footbridges and steps.
Start/Finish: Anchor Street, Coltishall, with roadside parking (TG279197);
BA moorings: Coltishall
Nearest Postcode: NR12 7AQ
Map: OS Explorer OL40 The Broads

Little
Hautbois

Mayton
Bridge

6

Mayton
Farm

Mayton Road

Bure Valley Path

10m

10m

River Bure

Great Hautbois Road

Great
Hautbois

The
Belt

10m

Fir
Hills

St Theobald's
(ruin) †

Castle
Wood

Church
Ponds

Buxton Road

Park
Farm

Largate
Farm

Colt's
Wood

†

B1354

Glebe Way

Norwi...

Read's
Hole

Cooper's
Grove

Horstead

10m

10m

N

B1150

Frettenham Road

0
¼ mile
½ mile
1 km

0
500 m

The route concludes with a walk along the Bure Valley Path for walkers and cyclists, which runs beside the narrow-gauge railway. The line also has stations at Brampton and Buxton.

To extend your visit, you can walk or take the Bure Valley Railway to Hoveton and Wroxham (either side of the Bure), where there's a Broads National Park information centre and wheelchair-accessible boat trips on solar-powered Ra.

Back at the common, around dusk, keep an eye out for a barn owl hunting over the meadows opposite.

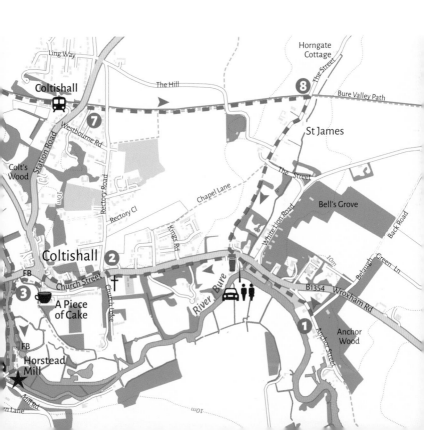

1 Walk across the common towards the pubs or follow the footpath by the road. Continue towards the centre of Coltishall on the footpath along Church Street.

2 After the church, cross the road with care to use the footpath and re-cross to the side with A Piece of Cake on it (actually a cafe!).

3 At the car park in front of the cafe, cross the green to the wooden footbridge. Turn left and follow the path by the river to the lock. Cross the bridge, turn left and then bear right towards Horstead Mill.

4 Cross the bridge over the mill-pool to the car park and turn right to walk upstream on the opposite bank of the river.

5 Cross Norwich Road with great care, making sure you can see oncoming traffic. Turn right and cross the bridge over the river, then turn left through a gate and follow the footpath by the river. Continue until you reach the Old Cromer Road at Mayton Bridge.

6 Turn right along the road and continue until you reach the road junction by the railway bridge. Turn right and shortly afterwards go down the steps on the left to join the Bure Valley Path. Turn right and walk beside the railway, continuing past Coltishall Station.

7 Continue until you pass farm buildings on the right and reach steps down to a road (The Street) just before bridge number 1295.

8 Turn right along the road (through the hamlet of St James) and continue until the road bends sharply left. Leave the road and follow the footpath in front of you. It will take you back to Church Street in Coltishall, opposite the pubs. Cross the road, turn left and retrace your steps to the starting point.

WALK 14

Ranworth, River Bure

This is a walk exploring a favourite Broads village.
There's lots to do if you want to spend the whole day here.

Car parking is available at the staithe, along with refreshments and toilets. You'll also find a Broads National Park information centre there, with an archive display about the history of Broads holidays. Ranworth has two broads, the one at the staithe is Malthouse Broad.

The walk includes a short woodland stretch with ancient oaks, as well as the mysterious carr or wet woodland approaching Ranworth Broad. You'll see all kinds of water birds on both broads. Birds to look out for at Ranworth Broad include common terns and visiting ospreys. Otters are also regularly seen there.

Norfolk Wildlife Trust's nature reserve (on the route) is open daily dawn to dusk, but no dogs, please. There's a visitor centre, floating on pontoons, with fantastic views of Ranworth Broad. As well as being great for birdwatching, the centre has all kinds of displays about the wildlife and history of the Broads. In summer, it can be a good place to see a swallowtail butterfly in the reeds nearby. The boardwalk and the visitor centre are accessible to wheelchair users. The trust offers boat trips on Ranworth Broad and a ferry service from the staithe.

You can also visit wonderful St Helen's Church, known as the cathedral of the Broads. It's famous for its rood screen and antiphoner – a beautiful illuminated service book written in Medieval Latin and produced around 1460 in Norwich. If you can climb up the church tower a bird's-eye view of the Broads awaits you. The church also has a visitor centre serving light refreshments.

Distance: 3.3 miles (5.3 km)
Time: 1½ hours
Terrain: Lanes, track, path and boardwalk.
Start/Finish: Ranworth Staithe, Ranworth (TG359146); BA moorings: Ranworth Staithe
Nearest Postcode: NR13 6HY
Map: OS Explorer OL40 The Broads

Back at the staithe, there are Broads National Park boat trips available on Liana, an Edwardian-style electric launch, going along the River Bure towards South Walsham. Look out for great crested grebes, even a kingfisher zipping across the water and look up too, a marsh harrier could be soaring overhead.

Slightly further afield by road, you can visit Fairhaven Woodland and Water Garden at South Walsham and Woodforde's Brewery at Woodbastwick (with tours available) – they are about 1½ and 2½ miles away.

1 With your back to the broad, turn left along Farm Lane, which becomes a track.

2 Follow the track as it turns right and right again, going through woodland.

3 At the gravel drive, follow the path as it turns left.

4 When you reach the lane, turn right up The Hill.

5 Turn left into Priory Road.

6 At the crossroads, turn right into Panxworth Church Road. Continue until you reach the crossroads at St Helen's Church, Ranworth.

7 Go ahead down Broad Road, with the church on your right.

8 Broad Road bends right. After the bend turn left into Norfolk Wildlife Trust's nature reserve.

9 A boardwalk leads to the trust's visitor centre.

10 Return to the lane (Broad Road) and turn left and then left again into Woodbastwick Road to return to the staithe.

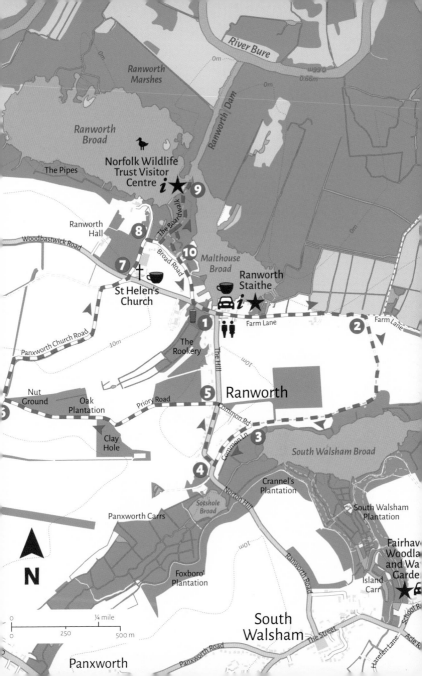

Medieval St Helen's Church at Ranworth, often referred to as the cathedral of the Broads

WALK 15

Upton, River Bure

There's a feeling of wildness here and despite the openness, the view seems to change quite rapidly.

This is a lovely walk, with both woodland and riverbank views. Look out for grebes on the water and lapwings on the marshes. You may also see marsh harriers, Chinese water deer, water voles, butterflies and dragonflies, including the Norfolk hawker. The whole area is managed for wildlife and there is grazing by cattle and sheep, so dogs should be kept on a lead.

You can go into Norfolk Wildlife Trust's nature reserve (please note, dogs are not allowed here), see its clear waters and explore its mysterious fen and woodland. It's another place that feels a bit of a hidden world of its own. The bird hide is a good vantage point.

You'll have views of several mills: Palmer's, St Benet's Abbey (and the abbey itself), St Benet's Level, Thurne, the Tall or Upton Black, Oby and Clippesby, and you'll get a real feel of how they influenced the landscape. Mills were sometimes named after the level or flat area of land they drained.

1 If you are arriving by car from Upton, the car park is on the left. From the car park walk alongside the boatyard, keeping Upton Dyke on your right.

2 Just after the boatyard take the first gate on your left. You'll see Palmer's Drainage Mill. Keep to the left-hand side of the field. The route takes you through a campsite.

Distance: 4.5 miles (7.3 km)
Time: 2½ hours
Terrain: Level walking, some uneven paths, can be wet and muddy, parts very exposed, gates.
Start/Finish: Upton Staithe car park, Boat Dyke Road, Upton (TG402128); moorings: Upton
Nearest Postcode: NR13 6BL
Map: OS Explorer OL40 The Broads

Thurne Dyke Windpump

The Street

Church Road

St Benet's
Level Mill

Pump
House
11

Boundary Road

Boundary
Farm

Oby

10

9

Upton Grazing
Marshes

River Bure

8 ★ Bird
Hide

12

7

6

The Marshman's
Cottage

Tall Mill

Oby

Upton Fen

Upton
Broad

5   FB

S Oby Dyke

4

Prince of Wales Road

Back Lane

3

Palmer's
Mill

Upton Dyke

Boat
Dyke Road

Marsh Road

The Green

Hanging Hill

Cargate Lane

Church Rd

Boat
Yard

1

2

Upton

Clipp
Mill

¼ mile   ½ mile
500 m   1 km

N

3 As you walk through the fields you'll go through two gates. At the third gate, a small wooden one to your left, go through and cross over a wooden footbridge on to a concrete track.

4 Turn right and follow the left-hand track round. You'll see a bridge on your left shortly.

5 Cross over the bridge and the second bridge. Turn right and the path will take you past carr (wet) woodland on your left and grazing marshes on your right.

6 Continue along the raised bank past two gates on your left.

7 Later, on the left, you'll see an entrance to Upton Fen. Explore the fen or continue straightaway along the embankment.

8 Continue past the second fen entrance. You'll also pass a bird hide where you may like to stop. Follow the path as it bears right and continue until you reach a gate on your right.

9 At the gate take the path that bears left (don't go through the gate). Continue along the path, following it as it turns left. Pass two gates on your right, then turn right between two hedgerows.

10 Go past the sluice on your left, keep left and head towards the brick pump house along the main track.

11 At the pump house, walk up on to the riverbank and turn right.

12 Continue along the river, passing the Tall Mill on your right, then continue along Upton Dyke to return to the car park.

WALK 16
Barton Broad, River Ant

Enjoy a panoramic view over the second largest of the broads.

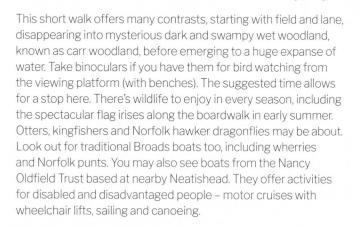

This short walk offers many contrasts, starting with field and lane, disappearing into mysterious dark and swampy wet woodland, known as carr woodland, before emerging to a huge expanse of water. Take binoculars if you have them for bird watching from the viewing platform (with benches). The suggested time allows for a stop here. There's wildlife to enjoy in every season, including the spectacular flag irises along the boardwalk in early summer. Otters, kingfishers and Norfolk hawker dragonflies may be about. Look out for traditional Broads boats too, including wherries and Norfolk punts. You may also see boats from the Nancy Oldfield Trust based at nearby Neatishead. They offer activities for disabled and disadvantaged people – motor cruises with wheelchair lifts, sailing and canoeing.

In the second half of the 20th century nitrate and phosphate levels increased and there was an abundance of algae, leading to a decline in other wildlife. Since the 1990s, the river water quality has steadily improved. Nutrient-enriched mud was pumped out of the broad and with improving water quality, fish and aquatic plants have made an impressive comeback, along with other species such as common terns.

The fen areas surrounding the broad are home to nationally rare plants including milk parsley. This is a scarce, vulnerable and declining plant, found mainly in East Anglian marshland. It is also the only food plant of the caterpillars of the swallowtail, Britain's largest butterfly.

Distance: 1.5 miles (2.4 km)

Time: 1 – 1½ hours

Terrain: Boardwalk section suitable for wheelchair users, with car park for disabled visitors at entrance. Boardwalk can be slippery in wet weather. Deep mud around boardwalk so do not step off it. Route from main car park via path and quiet lane.

Start/Finish: Barton Broad Boardwalk main car park, Long Road, Irstead (TG351208); car park for disabled visitors, Irstead Road, Irstead (TG359205); BA moorings: Gay Staithe, Irstead (about 5 minutes' walk to main car park) or the staithes at Irstead and Neatishead (about 15-20 minutes' walk)

Nearest Postcode: NR12 8XP

Map: OS Explorer OL40 The Broads

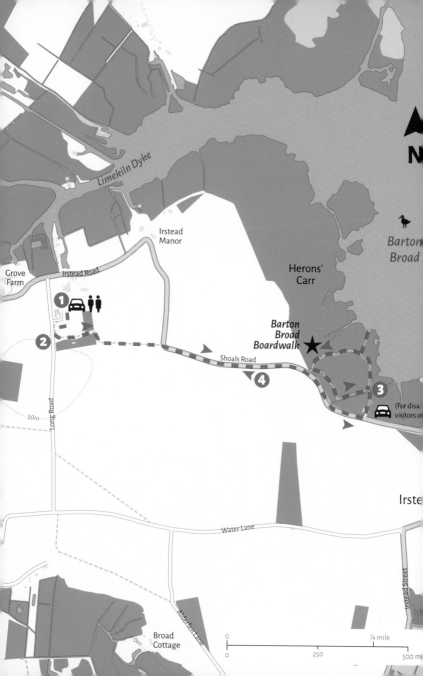

Limekiln Dyke

Grove
Farm

Irstead
Manor

Irstead Road

Herons'
Carr

Barton
Broad

**Barton
Broad
Boardwalk** ★

Shoals Road

(For disa
visitors o

Long Road

10m

Water Lane

Irste

Broad
Cottage

Attlefen Lane

Irstead Street

0
0   250   500 m

¼ mile

The Broads National Park supports one of the most extensive areas of lowland fen habitat in the UK, much of it here in the Ant Broads and Marshes Site of Special Scientific Interest (SSSI). Barton and How Hill (not far away down the River Ant) are two of the four nature reserves within this SSSI. Together the reserves support most of the UK conservation priority species associated with this habitat, including the largest colony of fen orchids and the highest density of swallowtail butterflies.

1 Barton Broad and Marshes is a Norfolk Wildlife Trust reserve, open every day, dawn till dusk. Assistance dogs only on the boardwalk please. There are accessible toilets in the main car park. Information panels will introduce you to the walk and there are resting places and tapping edges along the boardwalk, and some information in Braille. The walk starts in the corner to the right of the main car park entrance as you turn in. The route is waymarked from here.

2 Follow the path beside a small wood and then fields until you reach a lane. Turn right along the lane and continue to the boardwalk entrance at the car park for disabled visitors, on your left.

3 The boardwalk offers a circular anti-clockwise route with an exit close to the entrance.

4 Retrace your route back to the main car park or return along the lanes.

WALK 17

How Hill and St Benet's Abbey, River Ant

The landscape on this walk through history can seem as though it has never changed, but lots of aspects of it are man-made. It's a lovely, varied walk through farmland, alongside rivers, reedbeds and grazing marshes.

How Hill is one of the highest points in the Broads, at all of 12 m above sea level. You'll notice how the river is often higher than the surrounding land, which constantly has to be drained, now using electric pumps, though you'll pass many drainage windmills that used to do this job.

In summer listen for skylarks and warblers along the riverbank. Marsh harriers could be swooping overhead, hares and deer could be running through the grass. In winter Bewick's and whooper swans are often grazing on the marshes. Bats and owls are around at dusk and at dawn birdsong fills the air.

You can explore the remains of the abbey, founded over a thousand years ago. It's the only monastery in England that Henry VIII did not close down. Even to this day the Bishop of Norwich is also the Abbot of St Benet's. The abbey is a Norfolk Archaeological Trust site and you can walk around the site during daylight hours.

Parking is available at How Hill, the Broads Authority's nature reserve, which offers plenty for a day out in itself. There's tiny Toad Hole Cottage to visit, a nature trail (good for swallowtail butterflies) and boat trips on the Electric Eel, plus the How Hill

Distance: 8.5 miles (13.7 km)
Time: 4 hours
Terrain: Footpaths, tracks, lanes.
Footpaths can be wet and muddy,
especially in winter. Slopes and gates.
Start/Finish: How Hill, Ludham
(TG372189); BA moorings: How Hill,
Horning Marshes (Ludham Bridge),
St Benet's Abbey
Nearest Postcode: NR29 5PG
Map: OS Explorer OL40
The Broads

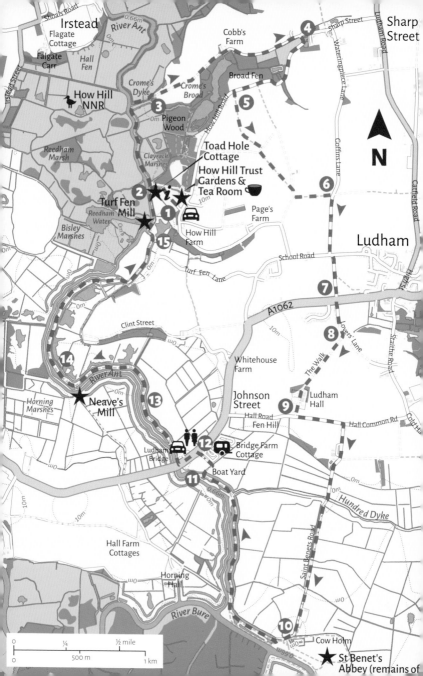

Trust's gardens and tea room. Assistance dogs only on the trail and boat trip please. The car park, with access to the riverside paths, is open all the time.

You can also start this walk from Ludham Bridge or St Benet's Abbey. Refreshments and toilets at Ludham, Ludham Bridge and How Hill.

1 Leave the car park and head across the green field towards a track. Turn left and follow the track down to the river.

2 Turn right to follow a path along the riverbank, passing Boardman's Mill and Clayrack Mill. Continue on the path as it bears right and then cross Crome's Dyke by turning left over the bridge.

3 Go ahead to the lane, an extension of Sharp Street. Turn right up the lane, which becomes a tarmac road. On your right you'll pass Crome's Broad (on the How Hill site).

4 At the first junction turn right along How Hill Road. Continue along this lane until a sign on your left shows the start of a path going uphill. Take this path.

5 Continue ahead with the hedge on your right as you enter the next field. When a footpath joins the track from your right (through the hedge) and the overhead power lines cross the path, a sign on the ground shows a path on your left. Follow this path to Goffins Lane.

6 Turn right down Goffins Lane and go almost straight ahead at the crossroads (crossing School Road) and continue along Pound Road to reach the A1062.

7 Take care crossing the road, then continue straight ahead along Lovers' Lane.

8 At the bottom of the hill take the signed path (The Walk) up the hill towards buildings (Ludham Hall and farm buildings). Continue ahead past the buildings to the road (Hall Road, becoming Hall Common Road).

9 Turn left, then take the next right. This byway takes you to St Benet's Abbey.

10 Turn right along the path as it follows the River Bure and then the River Ant towards Ludham Bridge.

11 Just before the bridge the path goes right, down a slope away from the river. Follow the path through a gate, around a field and through another gate to reach the A1062 again.

12 Cross the road carefully and turn left towards the bridge. Just before it, turn right alongside the moorings.

13 The footpath continues along the riverside.

14 After passing Neave's Mill on the opposite bank you can see Turf Fen Mill and How Hill ahead. The footpath moves away from the river but then returns to How Hill Staithe.

15 Walk along the staithe (beside the moorings) to the first turning on the right, leading to Toad Hole Cottage. Continue past the cottage up the slope and you'll see the car park slightly to the right.

A traditional Norfolk wherry passes a mill. Keels and trading wherries were used on the Broads for hundreds of years to transport cargoes around the region. Later, pleasure wherries and wherry yachts were built.

WALK 18

Horsey Mere, River Thurne

Combined with the activities and refreshments on offer and including extended walking if you wish, this could easily become a day trip.

The varied landscape is a mixture of waterways, marshland and farmland. Horsey is internationally important for wildlife and in winter the mere is a refuge for water birds, including thousands of geese who arrive from their northern breeding grounds. Lots of other birds may be seen, including willow and sedge warblers, hobbies, kestrels, marsh harriers, reed buntings, skylarks, stonechats, swans and greylag geese. In the summer look out for swallowtail butterflies (they like the wildlife garden at the start of the walk). Dogs are welcome on leads.

The National Trust's Horsey Windpump is open to visitors (61 steps) and there are great views from the top. There's also an exhibition about the history of the building. For a short walk, take the wheelchair-accessible route from the windpump for a wonderful view over the mere. The trust has a tea room at the staithe and there are toilets with access for disabled visitors.

On the walk described you'll also pass Brograve Mill, which dates from 1771 and was built to drain the Brograve Levels into Waxham New Cut. In the village, you can visit the lovely 13th-century All Saints' Church, with its thatched roof and round tower. The churchyard is full of snowdrops early in the year. Wildlife boat trips are available at the staithe from a separate operator.

If you extend your walk and continue past the Nelson Head pub you can take the path to the coast, with the chance to see seals on the beach in the winter months.

Distance: 3 miles (5 km)
Time: 1½–2 hours
Terrain: Level walk; uneven paths, narrow in places, muddy in wet weather; lanes. Separate route suitable for wheelchair users.
Start/Finish: National Trust car park (open dawn till dusk) at Horsey Windpump (TG456223); moorings: Horsey Staithe
Nearest Postcode: NR29 4EF
Map: OS Explorer OL40 The Broads

Fir Tree Farm

Waxham Road

Brograve Mill

③

④ Horsey Corner

FB

⑤ Delph Farm

Palling Road

Hills View

Waxham New Cut

All Saints' Church ✝ Horsey

⑥

All Saints Lane

⑦

Ne H

The Str

FB

Floating Meadow

FB

⑧

Mill Cottage

② Horsey Staithe

Horsey Mere

① Horsey Windpump

Horsey Road

N

0   ¼ mile

0   250   500

1 From the car park, walk past the toilet block to the dyke and turn right along the path.

2 Continue following this path as it winds along, follows Waxham New Cut and reaches Brograve Mill.

3 Turn right through farmland and follow the path until it reaches a lane, known as Horsey Corner.

4 Turn right, then immediately left on to a footpath. Follow this path through the fields until you reach a hedge in front of you.

5 Turn right here and follow the path with the hedge on your left until you reach the church.

6 At the church, turn left along All Saints Lane and then right to reach Horsey Road.

7 Take care crossing this road and then turn right. Follow the verge carefully along the left-hand side of the road for about 450 m until you come to a field opening with a track on your left.

8 Take the track (a permissive route) and continue straight ahead. Cross a footbridge and then turn right. Cross the road carefully to get back to the car park.

WALK 19
Potter Heigham, River Thurne

This is a peaceful walk with wetland views and lots of wildlife.

Enjoy the view of the partly thatched church, it dates from the 12th century and many original features remain. Have a look too at the last eel sett in the Broads, a small hut where an eel fisherman lived and where nets would be spread out across the river to catch the eels. In Victorian times eels were in great demand in London. They were kept alive in an eel trunk in the river before being taken for sale.

This whole area is rich in wildlife – marsh harriers, oyster catchers, spoonbills, egrets, ducks, swans, herons, greylag geese, cormorants and even cranes are among the birds you may see, as well as otters, deer, dragonflies and butterflies, including the rare swallowtail. The best time for swallowtails is June, with sometimes a second brood in August. Hickling, the largest of the broads, is not far away, and Hickling Broad and Marshes is a Norfolk Wildlife Trust nature reserve.

Hickling was also the site of the Broads Authority's CANAPE project (Creating A New Approach to Peatland Ecosystems), which was all about restoring wetlands and developing wetland agriculture. A hectare of reedbed is being restored on the south-west edge of the broad, based on aerial photos from 1946, with an adjacent still water refuge area for water birds. The project also trialled and promoted commercial products made from waste arising from conservation work, such as charcoal and compost. These products will reduce the cost of managing peatlands for nature.

Distance: 3.7 miles (6 km)
Time: 2½ hours
Terrain: Mainly flat footpaths, bridleways and quiet lanes. Some uneven, wet and muddy areas. Slopes, gates and steps.
Start/Finish: Small parking area by St Nicholas' Church, Church Lane, Potter Heigham (TG419198)
Nearest Postcode: NR29 5LL
Map: OS Explorer OL40 The Broads

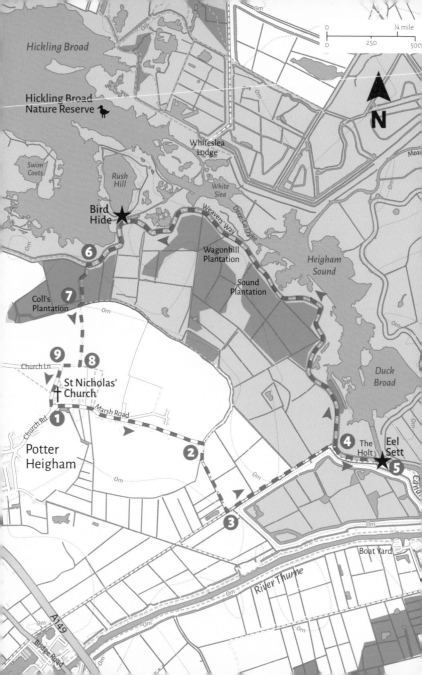

If you want to walk further you can continue on the Weavers' Way in either direction and if you'd like to see the Broads from the water, Potter Heigham is one of the many places in the Broads where you can hire day boats and canoes.

1 With the church behind you, turn left along Marsh Road and continue to the end of it.

2 Turn right on to a bridleway and continue until you reach a T-junction.

3 Turn left along a track, with a wetland area with reeds on the right.

4 At the end of the track, walk up some steps to a Weavers' Way signpost. Turn right for a detour to the eel sett on Candle Dyke.

5 Leave the eel sett, turn back and retrace your steps to proceed along the Weavers' Way.

6 After passing a Norfolk Wildlife Trust bird hide you'll come to another Weavers' Way signpost. Turn left across a footbridge, going over a dyke and into a wooded area.

7 The path leads to a junction by an information board. Turn right and continue on the path.

8 When you see the church turn right on to a bridleway and continue until you reach the lane.

9 Turn left on to Church Lane to return to the church.

An aerial view of Hickling Broad,
the largest of the broads and a
true wildlife haven

WALK 20

Winterton-on-Sea, River Thurne area

At Winterton you can explore the Broads and the coast.

Norfolk has some of the best examples of coastal sand dunes in the world, from Great Yarmouth, just south of here, all the way to The Wash in West Norfolk. With Great Yarmouth close by, Winterton is also one of the villages from where, in former times, local people set out in search of the silver darlings or herring. There are refreshments, shops and toilets.

If you go on to the beach, please follow the main route from the car park and don't go down the dunes. Take care walking on the beach and especially if you go in the sea.

On this walk, you'll see the impressive Holy Trinity and All Saints' Church, Horsey Windpump in the distance, St Mary's Church ruins, World War Two tank traps, and Winterton Dunes National Nature Reserve and Site of Special Scientific Interest.

There are no opening restrictions at the reserve but keep dogs on a lead. In the summer, adders may be present. The reserve shows good coastal habitat succession from the open sand and shingle beach, through dunes to heathland, low-lying wet areas and scattered scrub. The temporary pools provide breeding sites for nationally important colonies of natterjack toads. Insects and flowers love the area and in August you'll see heather. There are rare, ground-nesting little terns on Winterton Ness, with an area fenced off for them during the summer. Other birds to look and

Distance: 5 miles (8.1 km)
Time: 2–2½ hours
Terrain: Level walk along sandy tracks, quiet lanes and uneven paths; not much shade.
Start/Finish: Beach car park, Winterton-on-Sea (TG498197)
Nearest Postcode: NR29 4DD
Map: OS Explorer OL40 The Broads

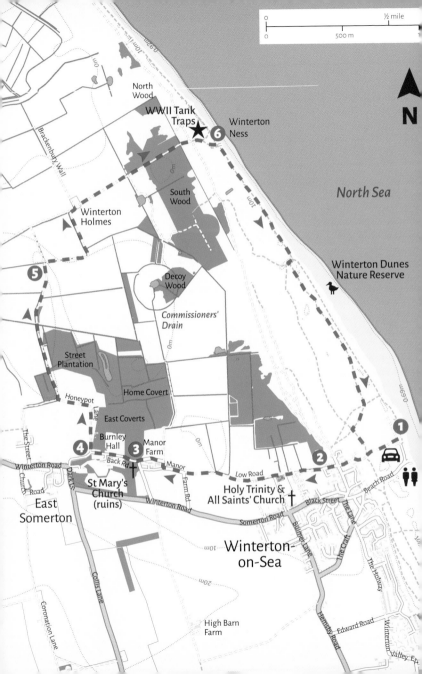

listen for on the walk include barn owls, buzzards, chiffchaffs, lapwings, stonechats and skylarks.

There is a large seal colony between Horsey and Winterton – seals have their pups on the beach in the winter. Keep at least 10 metres away from the seals and keep dogs on a lead.

1 If you're parking, check the closing time for the beach car park. Start at the far end of the car park, near the wooden boatsheds. With your back to the beach, follow the main sandy track opposite, going straight ahead, towards the church (there's a sign directing you).

2 At the end of a row of houses, go along Low Road, opposite. Low Road becomes a track and then joins Manor Farm Road going past Manor Farm.

3 Just past Manor Farm go straight ahead on the concrete road. You'll see the ivy-clad church ruins on your left. Continue on your way, passing the back of Burnley Hall, which dates from the early 1700s.

4 Just after the hall, take the concrete road round to the right, heading into the Burnley Estate. It continues past arable land and woodland, before opening out into grazing marshes.

5 Leave the concrete road, following the public footpath signs to the right, left and right, following a farm track zigzagging past farm buildings, and going through woodland and into the Winterton Dunes reserve.

6 At the tank trap blocks turn immediately right and follow the lower paths (not the top of the dunes) back to Winterton.

Norfolk has some of the most impressive sand dunes and loveliest beaches in the country—Winterton is a great example of both

Acknowledgements

Thanks to all of the photographers who allowed us to use their imagery in this book.

Page 6 © James Bass, page 10 © Bill Smith, page 15 © Jackie Dent, page 19 © Tom Barrett, page 23 © Tom Barrett, page 25 © Bill Smith, pages 28–29 © Bill Smith, page 31 © Tom Barrett, page 35 © James Bass, page 39 © James Bass, page 43 © James Bass, page 45 © Chris Herring, page 49 © Tom Mackie, page 51 © James Bass, page 55 © James Bass, page 57 © Tom Barrett, page 63 © Tom Barrett, page 66–67 © Tom Barrett, page 69 © Julian Claxton, page 73 © Tom Mackie, pages 76–77 © Chris Herring, page 79 © Tom Mackie, pages 82–83 © Chris Herring, page 85 © Tom Barrett, page 89 © Tom Barrett, page 91 © Julian Claxton, pages 94–95 © Julian Claxton, page 97 © Joanna Millington, pages 100-101 © Joanna Millington, page 103 © Bill Smith, page 107 © Chris Herring, page 111 © Bill Smith, page 113 © Julian Claxton, page 117 © James Bass, pages 120–121 © Mike Page, page 123 © Bill Smith, pages 126–127 © Bill Smith

Maps © OpenStreetMap contributors
Contains OS data © Crown copyright [and database right] 2021.
Map creation: Cosmographics Ltd (www.cosmographics.co.uk).
Page design and layout: mapuccino (mapuccino.com.au).